MR. KNOW IT ALL'S
GUIDE TO REAL ESTATE

JAHAN EPPS

Mr. Know it All's Guide to Real Estate

First edition. December 18, 2020

Edited by Bridgette Roche

For inquiries, email us at:

JayEppsRealty@gmail.com

To my Family, Friends and Batgirl for the inspiration

CONTENTS

SECTION 1

HOW TO BUY

STEP 1: PRE-QUALIFICATION

PRE-QUALIFICATION - a process whereby a loan officer takes information from a borrower and makes a tentative assessment of how much the lending institution is willing to lend them.

In order to prepare for this process, you must follow these steps:

A. Connect with Lender

LENDER - an individual, a public or private group, or a financial institution that makes funds available to another with the expectation that the funds will be repaid. Repayment will include the payment of any interest or fees.

B. Understand Mortgage Types

1. Conventional - A conventional mortgage or conventional loan is a home buyer's loan that is not offered or secured by a government entity. It is available through or guaranteed by a private lender or the two government-sponsored enterprises—Fannie Mae and Freddie Mac.

2. FHA - An FHA insured loan is a US Federal Housing Administration mortgage insurance backed mortgage loan that is provided by an FHA-approved lender. Requirements are not as stringent as traditional loans. FHA loans are designed for low-to-moderate- income borrowers; they require a lower minimum down payment and lower credit scores than many conventional loans.

C. Items Needed to Qualify

1. Credit Report - used to verify credit score and expenses. Debt from your credit report WILL be included in your debt used to calculate your (DTI) debt-to-income ratio

2. 30 days Pay stub - used to verify income and as proof of a steady job and pay. Also used to calculate debt-to-income (DTI)

3. Any other sources of income

- Pension
- SSI
- Dividends

4. 2 years tax return, W2 or 1099 if self-employed - overview of your yearly income and expenses as reported to the IRS, will be matched up with credit report and pay stubs for accuracy

5. 60 days bank statements - This shows proof of available capital and reserves. It will also be looked over for monthly expenditures, pay check deposits, rental deposits etc. The bank will also check bank statement for seasoning

- SEASONING – *the required amount months/time the money needs to be sitting/accumulating to be used in Real Estate transaction. This requirement is to avoid money laundering and is usually 2-6 months*

6. Lease agreements - If client has rental income- rental agreements are more proof of your income and rental amount should match deposit amounts on associated bank statement.

D. Qualification - What is the Bank Looking For?

1. Credit Score 680 and up - credit report

2. Enough Income to cover debt listed on credit <u>report</u> - Pay stubs, W2s, Credit report. – used to calculate *DTI*

3. Reserves – Bank statements

Note: Total debt should equal 50% or less of total income

PRE-QUALIFICATION IS COMPLETE WHEN YOU RECEIVE CONDITIONAL APPROVAL

———

STEP 2: SEARCH FOR YOUR HOME

A. Search Methods

1. MLS - Agents and brokers have access to MLS and can send listings

2. Other Internet search engines

- Zillow
- Redfin
- Trulia

3. Foreclosure List – public information, list can be received from multiple sources

- Private company- Craigslist, Facebook, etc.
- Title Company
- County Assessor's Office- search through assessor and recorder offices around the country by county, in a state-by-state directory, to help you find public records for properties in your area.

B. Auctions

Tax Sale - the **sale** of a real estate property that results when a taxpayer reaches a certain point of delinquency in his or her owed property **tax** payments.

Foreclosure - The purpose of a **foreclosure auction** is to get the highest possible price for the property, in order to mitigate the losses a lender suffers when a borrower defaults on a loan.

Standard Auction - there are 3 types of auctions:

1. Absolute Auction (or auction without reserve)

- The property is sold to the highest bidder, regardless of the price.
- Since a sale is guaranteed, buyer excitement and participation are heightened.
- Generates maximum profit
- Many sellers, including financial institutions and government agencies have begun to use this method more frequently.

2. Minimum Bid Auction

- The auctioneer will accept bids at or above a published minimum price. This minimum price is always stated in the brochure and advertisements and is announced at the auction.
- Reduced risk for seller as the sales price must be above a minimum acceptable level.
- Buyers know they will be able to buy at or above the minimum.
- The seller may, however, limit interest in the auction to only those buyers willing to pay the minimum bid price, and therefore it must be low enough to act as an inducement rather than a hindrance.

3. Reserve Auction (an auction subject to Confirmation)

In this scenario, the high bid is reduced, into an offer not a sale. A minimum bid is not published, and the seller reserves the right to accept or reject the highest bid within a specified time -- anywhere from immediately following the auction up to 72 hours after the auction concludes. Sellers predetermine the price at which the property will be sold and are not obligated to confirm a sale other than at a price that is entirely acceptable to them. The main disadvantage of a Reserve Auction is that prospective buyers may not invest the time and expense of due diligence when there is no certainty, they will be able to buy the property even if they are the highest bidder.

**Once you find the property of your choice, proceed to writing the offer

―――――

STEP 3: THE OFFER

Your offer should be competitive in nature and written in a way to give maximum chance at having offer accepted.

A. What Makes an Offer Competitive?

1. Purchase Price/Offer Price - If purchase price is reasonable offer should be within 5% in order to be competitive.

2. Contract Length/Days needed to close – 30 days or less most competitive

3. Deposit Amount/EMD - should be minimum 3%

4. Escrow/Title - The buyer or the buyer's real estate agent usually **suggest** the **escrow company**. The seller can agree to the buyer's selection or counter with another choice. The deciding factor usually depends on if it's a buyer or seller's market.

5. Contingencies - Contingencies are "walk-away" clauses in a contract that allow you to back out of buying a house if certain conditions aren't met. These contract stipulations serve both sides of a real estate transaction — protecting you as a buyer and protecting the seller, too. Fewer contingencies or shorter contingency periods are more competitive.

6. Financing

- All cash- Buyer offers to pay "All Cash" to purchase the property.
- Conventional- A conventional mortgage is a

home loan that isn't backed by a government agency, such as the FHA or VA. Conventional mortgage borrowers typically make larger down payments than FHA borrowers, and they tend to have a more secure financial standing and are less likely to default.

- FHA- government backed loan geared towards low-to-moderate income buyers and offers low down payment.
- Hard Money/Private- A hard money loan is a type of asset-based financing option. Asset-based financing means that the loan is secured by the equity or value of the property.

7. **Credits** – credits can be given to either side but usually the buyer receives. It is money credited to the balance for the benefit of the one receiving the credit

- Repair- credit given in lieu of making agreed upon repairs between buyer and seller.
- NRCC's- Non-Recurring Closing Cost are fees that are paid once, usually at a real-estate closing. Closing costs can include origination fees, appraisal costs, points, and title insurance. Credits can also be given to the buyer or seller to cover a portion or all NRCCs. Buyer usually receives

———

STEP 4: ESCROW

Escrow – a contractual arrangement in which a third party receives and disburses money or property for the primary transacting parties, most generally, used with plentiful terms that conduct the rightful actions that follow. The disbursement is dependent on conditions agreed to by the transacting parties. (once executed/signed by both parties, thereby being accepted) **Escrow is a mutual 3rd party hired to oversee and facilitate the real estate transaction.**

A. Open Escrow - Money goes to an objective third party until all terms are agreed upon and finances are cleared.

B. Title Report and Insurance – Insurance Company which ensures the appropriate parties with authority to execute transaction are available and present. If fraud happens after escrow Title insurance covers.

1. **Title Report**- A title report is a document that outlines the legal status of a property and related information on its ownership.

2. **Title Insurance** - protects you from financial loss and related legal expenses in the event there is a defect in title to your property that is covered by the policy. In California, there are two types of title insurance policies.

- **CLTA** (California Land Title Association) policy insures the property owner.
- **ALTA** (American Land Title Association) is an extended coverage policy that insures the lender against possible unrecorded risks excluded in the CLTA policy.

**The CLTA title insurance coverage remains active until the property is sold, while the ALTA lender's policy remains in place until the loan is paid off.

C. Obtain the Home Inspection – attempts to find any default in the property to give buyer an accurate depiction of property's condition past the interior walls. (Usually, last time to ask for repair credits)

D. Appraisal - establishes value of the property (must be equal to purchase or more if financed.)

E. Secure Financing - Lender

F. Approve the Seller Disclosures - California, like many states, requires its residential property sellers to disclose, in writing, details about the property they have on the market. The disclosures are important so potential buyers can know as much as possible about a properties defects before purchasing the property.

G. Purchase Hazard Insurance – almost any insurance carrier of your choice will do

H. The Final Walk-Through – verify property is in condition as expected usually done right before funding or recording.

———

STEP 5: CONTINGENCIES

CONTINGENCIES -"walk-away" clauses in a contract that allow you to back out of buying a house if certain conditions aren't met.

A. Inspection – usually lasts 10 – 17 days – allows you to ask for repairs or credits to cure and/or walk away if agreement cannot be made.

1. **Home Inspection-** Hire an inspector (usually by Realtor recommendation) to check the property.

2. **Pest Inspection-** This will check for termites, rodents, etc. and is separate from the home inspection.

B. Loan – usually 17 – 21 days – time to secure approval for finance or walk away without penalty

C. Appraisal – usually 17 days – allows you and lender time to establish real value of the property if price too high, price can be reduced or buyer/seller may walk away without penalty

———

STEP 6: LOAN PROCESS

A. Full Submission – When all necessary docs have been submitted to underwrite the loan.

1. Lock in lowest interest rate with the help of a lender before signing papers.

B. **Appraisal**- report detailing the estimated value of the property

C. PTD- Prior-to-Docs conditions or sometimes referred to as PTD are conditions the underwriter requires before the loan documents can be ordered.

D. PTF- Prior-to-Funding conditions are conditions that come up after an underwriter reviews the loan. These conditions must be met before the loan will be funded by the lender.

―――

STEP 7: CLOSING

A. Final Walkthrough- walk the property one last time to ensure there's nothing that could violate terms.

B. Recording - Making record of new deed transferring ownership

SECTION 2

HOW TO SUBMIT AN OFFER

STEP 1: SUBMIT OFFER W/ CLIENT'S TERMS

Parts of an Offer

1. **Offer** – usually written on C.A.R (California Association of Realtors) form

2. **Conditional Approval-** Conditional Approval proves we can purchase for the price offered.

3. **Bank Statement-** Proves down payment

4. **Credit Report(optional)**

———

STEP 2: CONFIRM WITH LISTING AGENT THAT EVERYTHING WAS RECEIVED

SECTION 3

SELLING

STEP 1: DEAL OR NO DEAL

First decide if it's the right time to sell. By using a lottery type scenario. I calculate my monthly rental income or potential rental income of the property. Then calculate my equity and current profit margin. Divide the profit / monthly rental income = the number of months it would take me to reach my profit margin, not considering expenses such as maintenance and evictions.

Example:

A. Calculate monthly rent $2,200

1. Assuming it's not already rented look up local rent in the area

B. Calculate equity and profit margin of potential sale $240,000

C. Refer to Property Valuation $500,000

Subtract 7% of the potential sales price to account for commission and closing cost

> *Sales price: $500,000*
> *Closing costs: - $35,000*
> **Max potential profit $465,000**

Subtract mortgage and any other liens and encumbrances

Max potential profit: $465,000
Mortgage & Liens: -$235,000
*Potential Net sales Profit: **$230,000***

Potential Sales Profit ÷ Monthly Sales Income

$235,000 ÷ 2200 = **106 months**

106 months ÷ 12 months in a year = 9 years to receive equal pay out

----

STEP 2: PICK AN AGENT

1. **Trustworthy** – Can be trusted to deliver truth and put forth due diligence and effort

2. **Knowledgeable** – Knows what they're doing and can perform

3. **Familiar with Area** – knows or specializes in specific market

4. **Network**- Has a strong Real estate network

STEP 3: MARKETING

1. **Broker Network** – underestimated source for good buyers

2. **Lawn Sign** – still best way to advertise for both visibility and cost

3. **Open House** – effective but tends to draw a lot of, "I'm just looking" traffic.

4. Mailers – good for generating future business, more so than current buyers

———

STEP 4: ANALYZING OFFERS

Purchase Price – How much are they offering?

A. EMD- Earnest money deposit – How much of a deposit are they risking to show their level on seriousness?

B. Down Payment – How much of the Purchase price are they putting down with personal funds?

C. Type of Financing – some forms of financing are more reliable than others

D. Contingencies- clauses which allow buyers to walk away from the escrow harmless. The more contingencies, the longer the time period they are in effect, the riskier the deal for the seller

E. Closing date - How much time buyer needs to close escrow?

F. Credits – ultimately take away from the seller's net proceeds, the fewer the better

G. Other Terms – check this section as it could contain additional stipulations, conditions, credits etc.

H. Escrow and Title – the party that chooses these services are a negotiation point as rapport could make the transaction smoother.

———

STEP 5: TITLE

A. Address Legal Issues- Check for any encumbrances and liens.

I. ENCUMBRANCES - *a claim against a property by a party that is not the owner.*

- An encumbrance can impact the transferability of the property and restrict its free use until the encumbrance is lifted. The most common types of encumbrance apply to real estate; these include mortgages, easements, and property tax liens.

2. **PROPERTY LIEN** - *a legal claim on assets that allows the holder to obtain access to the property if debts are not paid.*

- A property lien must be filed and approved by a county records office or state agency.

B. Who Chooses?

1. Negotiable

2. Usually determined by who has favor in the market; buyer or seller

———

STEP 6: CONTINGENCIES

A. Inspection – gives buyers time to do a thorough investigation of the condition of the property inside and out, top to bottom. Any issues with the condition of the property of repairs requested must be brought for in this time. If period expires buyer must sign to go forward or cancel. Unless damage occurs after or a reasonable effort to hide damage was made or undisclosed.

B. Appraisal- gives buyers' and buyer's lender time to substantiate the purchase price, in hopes that the purchase price is of equal or lesser amount than the appraisal amount.

C. Loan – gives buyers and buyers lender time to get buyer approved for finance

D. Other- for instance, will the property be delivered vacant or will appliances be included

―――――

STEP 7: REQUESTS THAT CAN BE MADE BY BUYERS DURING ESCROW

A. Repairs – for defects to be repaired before close of escrow, credit can be given in lieu

B. Credits – Can be for closings costs, repairs, rents, seller leaseback

C. Extensions – time extended for any contingencies or closing date may be requested

D. **Disclosure** – Buyers can ask for disclosure of any known material fact based upon inspection and discovery

―――――

STEP 8: FUNDING

When all buyers conditions have been met, their lender will clear the loan for funding.

A. Buyer will receive DU approval

A DU presents a fairly complete financial picture of the borrower. It is one way to make yourself distinguishable by showing the seller you have the money and are qualified to buy the property.

Approval will have to meet conditions needed prior to loan docs.

B. Loan Docs

- Note ("IOU")
- Deed of Trust ("Security Agreement" or "Lien Doc")
- Grant Deed
- Riders
- Lending Instructions
- Escrow Contract Amendments
- Closing Disclosure (CD)

C. Bank funds the loan

The bank will wire the money needed to fund the transaction in order to pay off debt needed to buy the house.

———

STEP 9: RECORD DEED

When you buy a home, it is usually the job of your title or escrow agent to file your original deed — the document showing that you legally own the property — in the appropriate government office in your county. This is called "recording" your deed.

SECTION 4

PROPERTY VALUATION

STEP 1: LOCATION

This is the most important factor in all cases.

———

STEP 2: COMPARABLE SALES

Are recent sales of similar homes in proximity to the subject property analyzed to establish a value for the subject property? Comparison method is the most common valuation method amongst residential appraisers.

A. Most important requirements to be considered:

1. .5-mile proximity from the subject property

2. Sold within 6 months of date of appraisal

3. Same bedroom and bath count

Also consider:

4. Square footage

5. Future development in the area

———

STEP 3: DESIRABLE FEATURES

Kitchen- usually the most desirable feature among families must be big enough and nice enough to make cooking for a family less of a task

Master Bedroom – where the income owners will spend most of their time

Master Bathroom – also where the owners spend most of their time

Bathroom – Common area seen by most guests also determines how fast dressing happens in morning

Master Closet – wives like big closets

Yard – for children to play safely or for enough room to add on

SECTION 5

FINANCING

STEP 1: TYPES

A. Conventional- A conventional mortgage or conventional loan is a home buyer's loan that is not offered or secured by a government entity. It is available through or guaranteed by a private lender or the two government-sponsored enterprises—Fannie Mae and Freddie Mac.

B. Commercial- A commercial real estate loan is a mortgage secured by a lien on commercial property as opposed to residential property. Commercial real estate (CRE) refers to any income-producing real estate that is used for business purposes; for example, offices, retail, hotels, and apartments.

C. Government Backed

1. **FHA**- A Federal Housing Administration (**FHA**) **loan**

 is a mortgage insured by the FHA that is designed for lower-income borrowers.

2. **VA**- A VA loan is a mortgage loan in the United States guaranteed by the United States Department of Veterans Affairs.

D. Sub Prime- Subprime loans are a category of loans with relatively high interest rates and fees that are offered to borrowers with less-than-ideal credit.

E. Hard Money- A hard money loan is a specific type of asset-based loan financing through which a borrower receives funds secured by real property. Hard money loans are typically issued by private investors or companies.

F. Private- Private money is a commonly used term in banking and finance. It refers to lending money to a company or individual by a private individual or organization.

G. Construction- A construction loan is a type of bank-issued short-term financing, created for the specific purpose of financing a new home or other real estate project.

———

STEP 2: QUALIFY FOR LOAN APPROVAL

A. Qualifications

1. **Credit** – should be 680 or above to qualify for top tier financing. Credit report will be run and analyzed for delinquencies and estimate of monthly expenses

2. **Income**- will be verified through 2 years tax returns and current pay check stubs. Must be at least 50% more than monthly expenses

3. **Capital**- liquid assets to cover costs of transaction and expenses for a 3-6 months

———

STEP 3: SUBMIT LOAN (AFTER PROPERTY HAS BEEN IDENTIFIED AND ESCROW OPEN)

A. Full Documentation- Items needed for submission:

1. Credit Report

2. Title Report

3. Purchase Contract

4. Appraisal

5. Proof of income

6. Pay stubs

7. Retirement or settlement award letters

8. Lease agreements for each tenant

9. Bank statements

10.Tax returns/w2s

B. Stated (state your information) – meaning bank will NOT ask for evidence to back up your financial claims. Easier to qualify usually comes with higher interest rate.

―――――

THE DOS & DON'TS DURING THE MORTGAGE PROCESS

While securing a loan can seem overwhelming, there are a few things you can do and a few things to avoid to make the loan process even easier.

Mortgage Process DOs & DON'Ts

DO	DON'T
DO Advise your lender if any information you provided CHANGES • Address • Job or salary • Any Info	**DON'T** Make ANY significant purchases during the mortgage process. It could negatively impact your debt-to-income ratio.
DO Keep records of ALL bank transactions, especially if you transfer large amounts from one account to another.	**DON'T** Consolidate credit cards or get ANY new lines of credit
DO Get homeowners insurance with coverage equal to the amount or replacement value of your home.	**DON'T** Pay off any collections or charge-offs. This can actually cause your credit score to drop.
DO Get termite inspection of the purchase property.	**DON'T** Change jobs if possible. It is more desirable to show two years' work history and a new job will affect that.
DO Protect your credit scores. You'll want to stay on top of any little change that may impact your loan.	**DON'T** Co-Sign for another borrower. This will show up as additional debt, and can affect your credit.
DO Talk to your loan agent if you have any questions or concerns about your loan.	**DON'T** Change your overall asset picture. This could include changing investments, opening/closing accounts, or making unexplained large deposits.

SECTION 6

REFINANCE

STEP 1: CALCULATE YOUR LOAN TO VALUE (LTV)

LOAN TO VALUE – *the most important factor when it comes to refinancing (should be less than .8 or 80% of total value)*

A. Loan amount desired

B. Calculate Value

C. Divide

Loan amount ÷ Property value = Loan to Value

———

STEP 2: UNDERSTAND YOUR CREDIT, INCOME, LIENS, AND COSTS

Credit is the next important factor then income, liens and costs.

A. Score

1. Do you pay people back?

- Are you refinancing because you are overwhelmed with debt – banks prefer loans to go to home improvement
- Lender will use debt listed to determine Debt to Income ratio (DTI)

Total debt ÷ Total Income = DTI

B. Income

Your lender wants to see you have enough income to keep up with timely payments

1. Pay stubs

2. Rental agreements

3. Benefits award letter

4. Delinquencies

5. Lender may require to be paid off

C. Liens

Liens will be made to be paid off at refinance

1. Tax

2. Mechanics

D. Costs

When calculating costs, it is most important to know how everyone is getting paid and what fees. It also helps to know what's negotiable and what's not.

1. **Loan Origination Fee**

- Points short for percentage points of the loan amount charged to the borrower for orchestrating the loan
- Usually charged by Mortgage Broker or Lender or both
- Negotiable

2. **Application Fee**

3. Appraisal Fee

- Fee paid to indecent appraiser for valuation of home by the **buyer.**
- Lender mandatory (any and all lenders require an appraisal)
- Non – Negotiable

4. Flood/Earthquake Certification Fee

5. Escrow

Neutral third party to facilitate agreement between **lender and borrower/buyer.**

- Paid to escrow
- Somewhat negotiable
- Homeowners' Insurance Fee
- Property Taxes

6. Title and Closing Fees

- Title Exam/ Closing Fee
- Title Insurance Premium
- Recording Fees
- Prorated Property Taxes
- Prorated HOA Dues, if applicable
- Attorney Fees – **Seller pays**

7. Real Estate Fees

- Real Estate Commissions
- Repair Costs, if applicable

8. Notary

9. Lender

- Underwriting fee

Closing Costs Explained

Buyer Costs	Seller Costs
Lender Fees •Origination Fee •Application Fee •Appraisal Fee •Flood/Earthquake Certification Fee •Discount Points* Escrow Charges •Homeowners' Insurance Escrows •Property Tax Escrows Title Exam/Closing Fee •Title Insurance Premium •Recording Fees •Prorated Property Taxes •Prorated HOA Dues*	Real Estate Fees •Real Estate Commissions •Repair Costs* Title & Closing Fees •Excise Tax (Revenue Stamps) •Attorney Fees (Deed & Doc Prep) •Prorated Property Taxes •Prorated HOA Dues* Miscellaneous Fees •Wire Fees •Home Warranty* •Buyer's Closing Costs* *if applicable

Be sure to factor in these closing costs.
Will usually be around 2-4% of purchase price

SECTION 7

FORECLOSURE

FORECLOSURE - *the beginning of the legal process of forced sale.*

STEP 1: NOTICE OF DEFAULT (NOD)

Begins after 3 months of delinquency

A. At this point, banks only are obligated to take full delinquent amount

B. Default on your mortgage becomes public information

1. Informs any other creditors or lien holders that collateral or assets that you own are at risk of loss and so is their lien

C. Ways to cure/ Stop the property from foreclosure sale.

1. **Sell** the property if you have enough equity

2. **Modification-** agreement with lender to change 1-3 terms which determine P&I (principal and interest) amount of a mortgage payment. TI (Tax and Insurance) are not determine by the lender but by government and insurance policy. Makes up total payment known as PITI

3. Forbearance- an agreement with the bank to split up the delinquent amount into payments over 6mos. – 2years to be paid in addition to current payment

4. Short sale - is a sale of real estate in which the net proceeds from selling the property will fall short of the debts secured by liens against the property.

5. Reinstatement- paying the amount pass due up until the time of judgment rendered by court.

6. Redemption - After judgement, pay the entire loan amount plus penalties, interest, and court cost.

7. Deed in lieu- A deed in lieu of foreclosure is a deed instrument in which a mortgagor (i.e. the borrower) conveys all ownership interest in a real property to the mortgagee (i.e. the lender) to satisfy a loan that is in default and avoid foreclosure proceedings.

STEP 2: NOTICE OF TRUSTEE SALE (NOT)

When the lender or trustee elects to sell (usually thru judicial Foreclosure) to recover collateral (home) used to secure the debt.

A. Ways to Cure

1. Sale - Provide a buyer before scheduled sale that will purchase for a price high enough to pay off all debts, this can be done until right before a Trustee sale

2. Bankruptcy – comes with an automatic stay on any filing on the property including foreclosure proceedings

3. Any option from above section C 1-7 but all information needs to be submitted to the bank within 30 days of trustee sale date

SECTION 8

LIENS AND ENCUMBRANCES

Liens and Encumbrances are items affecting ownership

STEP 1: TITLE

TITLE - *a document that lists the legal owner of a piece of property and all debt (liens) attached to it. Titles can be issued to depict ownership of both personal and real property.*

A. Lien - *a form of security interest granted over an item of property to secure the payment of a debt or performance of some other obligation. The owner of the property, who grants the lien, is referred to as the lienee and the person who has the benefit of the lien is referred to as the lien or lien holder*

1. **Mortgage Lien**- A mortgage lien is a form of conditional ownership of your property claimed by your home loan provider.

2. **Mechanic's Lien** – A lien created by statute which exists against real property in favor of persons who have performed work or furnished materials for the improvement of the real property.

3. **General Lien** – A lien on all the property of a debtor.

4. **Specific Lien** – A lien that attaches to one specific property only.

5. **Package Loan**– A type of loan used in home financing covering real property, improvements, and movable equipment/appliances.

6. **Judgment Lien** – A legal claim on all of the property of a judgment debtor which enables the judgment creditor to have the property sold for payment of the amount of the judgment.

7. **Junior Mortgage** - is a mortgage that is subordinate to a first or prior (senior) mortgage. A junior mortgage often refers to a second mortgage, but it could also be a third or fourth mortgage (e.g. home equity loans or lines of credit (HELOCs)).

*LIS PENDENS - *a written notice that a lawsuit has been filed concerning real estate, involving either the title to the property or a claimed ownership interest in it.*

*ENCUMBRANCE- any charge, claim, right, burden (otherwise called a cloud on title), and/or interest in real property other than the owners, including but not limited to, any restriction upon the title to real property, affecting and/or limiting any interests or its use.

*EASEMENT - *a right, privilege or interest limited to a specific purpose which one party has in the land of another.*

B. CC&Rs- Covenants, Conditions and Restrictions

Covenants, conditions, and restrictions (also called "CC&Rs") are used by many "common interest" developments, including condominiums and co-ops, to regulate the use, appearance, and maintenance of property. CC&Rs, most commonly drafted and enforced through homeowners' associations (HOAs), often restrict what homeowners can do on their property.

———

STEP 2: HOW TO CLEAR TITLE

Clear Title is the phrase used to state that the owner of real property owns it free and clear of encumbrances.

Cloud Title - A cloud on title is any document, claim, unreleased lien, or encumbrance that might invalidate or impair a title to real property or make the title doubtful. Clouds on the title are usually discovered during a title search.

Two ways to clear title:

A. Settle - agree to and pay lien or debt to solve, done through negotiation and payment

B. Dispute

1. Usually requires a bond for the amount in question

SECTION 9

HOW TO INVEST

STEP 1: IDENTIFY WHAT TYPE OF INVESTOR YOU WANT TO BE

A. Long term- Buy and Hold

B. Short Term- Fix and Flip

———

STEP 2: DETERMINE WHAT TYPE OF FINANCING YOU WILL HAVE

A. Personal funds

B. Cash

1. **Hard Money-** a way to borrow without using traditional mortgage lenders. Loans come from individuals or investors who lend money based (for the most part) on the property you're using as collateral. The hard money loan is considered asset-based financing meaning that the loan is secured by the equity or value of the property.

2. **Group-** money pooled together by a group of investors or individuals

3. **Crowd Funding-** the practice of funding a project or venture by raising small amounts of money from a large number of people, typically via the Internet.

―――――

STEP 3: DETERMINE THE TYPE OF PROPERTY

A. Single Family Residence

i. Much safer for beginners, hardest to determine ARV

B. Luxury Home

i. Most expensive, not for beginners, must have luxury fixtures which are

expensive

C. Multi Unit

i. Usually for long term investment and/or residual income

―――――

STEP 4: RENOVATION

A. Calculate Construction Time – best estimate for a novice is to ask a couple experts/builders and make an educated guess

B. Calculate Construction Costs – recommend using a construction calculator to itemize the costs. Then line item audit the estimate based on more accurate knowledge

C. Interview Contractors and Repairmen

D. Calculate permit costs – LADBS will usually tell you directly or give you the website to DIY

―――――

STEP 5: RESALE

A. Pitfalls

1. **Paid too much on the purchase** – you make you money on the buy not the sale. Spending too much money on the property is a problem that is rarely fixed.

2. **Out Built the neighborhood** - don't build a high rise or mansion on Baltic Ave (low income area). You cannot get the appropriate value for what you put in, much more common than one might think

3. **High Construction Costs** – this is your biggest expense every time, mismanagement of this can be your biggest downfall

4. **Unnecessary or useless renovations** – add little to no value and adds to your overall construction costs

5. **Miscalculation of time to execute project – Time IS money.** The longer the project the more the cost

6. **Bad Investors – an uneducated investor is your worst friend,** and sometimes in litigation can be an enemy. Do not underestimate the importance of an educated investor even if you have to educate them.

SECTION 10

HOW TO INCORPORATE

STEP 1: DETERMINE WHAT TYPE OF ENTITY YOU WANT TO FORM?

LLC is the most typical entity used for Real Estate investing

A. How many units? When investing as a group LLC is broken into units(shares) and assigned based on amount invested.

B. What activities will the entity be doing specifically?

C. How will the business or entity be managed?

―――

STEP 2: HOW DO YOU WANT TO BE TAXED?

A. Individually (C- Corp)- The biggest difference between C and S corporations is taxes. C corporations pay tax on their income, plus you pay tax on whatever income you receive as an owner or employee. An S corporation doesn't pay tax. Instead, you and the other owners report the company revenue as personal income.

A. Collectively (S-Corp)- S corporations are corporations that elect to pass corporate income, losses, deductions, and credits through to their shareholders for federal tax purposes. Shareholders of S corporations report the flow-through of income and losses on their personal tax returns and are assessed tax at their individual income tax rates. This allows S corporations to avoid double taxation on the corporate income

———

STEP 3: HOW TO HOLD TITLE?

A. Trust

B. LLC

C. Personal Name

SECTION 11

CONSTRUCTION

This is the most important factor in terms of Accuracy. ARV is short for after repair value, or the estimate of a property's value after all repairs and upgrades are completed. ARV= Property's Current Value + Value of Renovations.

A. Pull Up Comps

I. Gather a minimum of 5 comparable homes based on improvements

- Similar bedroom/ bathroom count
- Similar square footage
- 0.5-mile radius
- Same area designation ie. Leimert Park, Jefferson Park

B. Zoning

I. Look up zoning of the potential property to see what improvements or additions are allowable.

- Setback requirements
- SFR vs Multi-unit zoning
- Parking requirements
- Historic designation

STEP 2: CONSTRUCTION CALCULATOR

You want to use a construction calculator to estimate the construction costs. Use one that will break down labor vs. materials and itemizes all expenses

A. Analyze the individual items to see what is relevant to your project and what isn't

B. Look to cut any unnecessary or overprice items.

1. Saving $200 on each item on a 50-item list would save $10K on a project

2. You can also save by shopping around for materials

3. Shop around for labor also

STEP 3: UNDERSTAND THE PROCESS

A. View DIY videos on YouTube to understand the labor involved in each building process

SECTION 12

HOW TO BE A LANDLORD

STEP 1: PROFITABILITY

Profitability is measured with income and expenses.

A. Income- how much money is being generated from the activities of the investment.

B. Expenses- cost of resources to maintain real estate investment.

1. Maintenance and repairs

- Plumbing
- Heating/AC
- Pest Control
- Landscape
- Common areas, walkways, stairwells, and railings

2. Utilities

- Water
- Trash
- Sewer
- Power

Annual income – Annual expenses = Property's value

NOTE: To determine ROI (Return on Investment) SEE BASICS OF CAP RATE

———

STEP 2: RENOVATIONS

Must be done from time to time to keep building up to date and maintain property value

———

STEP 3: RESIDUAL INCOME

The amount of net income generated in excess of the minimum rate of return. Residual income can be used to describe the amount of net income after all costs are paid down, it also refers to the amount of money you continue to generate after your initial work is done.

———

STEP 4: MAINTENANCE

Regular repairs and upkeep must be done on the property to keep it up to code.

———

STEP 5: EVICTION

EVICTION - *the removal of a tenant from rental property by the landlord. In some jurisdictions it may also involve the removal of persons from premises that were foreclosed by a mortgagee.*

7 STEPS TO **Evict a Tenant in California**

1. DETERMINE LEGAL GROUNDS FOR EVICTION

- Fail to pay rent
- Break the lease or breach another term of the rental agreement
- Commit waste (for example, by damaging the property)
- Become a serious nuisance to other tenants
- Conduct illegal activity on the property

2. PROVIDE THE TENANT WITH NOTICE

- Personally, delivering a copy of the notice to the tenant
- Leaving the notice with an adult person at the tenant's residence
- Obtaining a court order to post the notice on the tenant's front door

3. FILE AN UNLAWFUL DETAINER LAWSUIT

One of the more detailed steps of evicting a tenant is completing the paperwork involved in the court process.

4. ALLOW THE TENANT TIME TO RESPOND OR VACATE PREMISES

Once you file your complaint, the court will issue a summons to the tenant. After the date of service of the civil eviction complaint, the tenant has five days to file a response or vacate the premises.

5. REQUEST A COURT DATE FOR TRIAL

If the tenant does not file an answer or respond to the court case within five days, you may be able to continue the process without a court trial. However, if the tenant does file an answer, you should immediately request a court trial date. Usually, a court trial is scheduled within 10-20 days of filing the request.

6. GO TO COURT

If the tenant does not leave within five days, request a court date from the judge. Before the court date, gather any and all legal documents relating to the rental, as well as physical proof of a failure to pay (e.g., bounced checks). This will help you prove your case against the tenant, and challenge any defense mounted by the tenant.

7. HAVE SHERIFF SCHEDULE MOVE OUT

One of the last steps in evicting a tenant in California is arranging the formal move out. If the judge rules in your favor, they will sign a court order that terminates the tenant's right to remain on the property.

The Basics of CAP RATE in Real Estate Investing

What is a cap rate?

Also known as capitalization rate, the cap rate is a return on investment metric.

How to calculate:

Cap Rate = Annual Net Operating Income (NOI) /Property Price

Example:

Property price = $200,000

Monthly Rental Income= $1,500

Annual Operating Costs = $5,000

Annual (NOI)= ($1,500 x 12)- $5,000 = $13,000

Cap Rate = $13,000/$200,000

= 6.5%

What affects cap rate?

1. Location
2. Type of Investment Property
3. Interest Rates

SECTION 13

PROBATE

This occurs when deceased passes and doesn't have the property secured in a trust, deed defeasible or joint tenant with the right of survivorship.

STEP 1: HIRE PROBATE ATTORNEY

A. Payment

Based on the value of the entire estate

Here are the current rates:

- 4% of the first $100,000 of the gross value of the probate estate
- 3% of the next $100,000
- 2% of the next $800,000
- 1% of the next $9 million
- .5% of the next $15 million

———

STEP 2: FILE PROBATE PROCEEDINGS

This will determine who are the heirs and whom has the authority to make and execute decisions on behalf of the estate.

STEP 3: DETERMINE ADMINISTRATOR

The Administrator has the power to make decisions and execute agreements on behalf of the estate.

A. Full Authority

Full authority means the ability to exercise the Governor's powers, responsibilities, obligations, and authorities as provided by general law and in the State Constitution without assuming the office of the Governor.

B. Limited Authority

Personal representative is able to take all other actions permitted under the rules of the IAEA. Court supervision is required over the administration of the estate not able to do the following without court involvement:

1. Sell the estate's real estate

2. Exchange the estate's real estate

3. Grant an option to purchase the estate's real estate

4. Borrow money by using the estate's real estate as collateral

------

STEP 4: SETTLE DEBT ON PROPERTY

A. Refinance – obtain new financing to replace old financing. If enough equity is present more money may be taken out to cover expenses, renovations, repairs or just to spend.

B. Sale – the most obvious way to pay off debts associated with property and estate.

SECTION 14

LITIGATION

Real estate litigation is a course of action that may be taken to resolve significant disputes dealing with residential or commercial property.

A. Judicial

1. **Lis Pendis**- a Lis pendens is a written notice that a lawsuit has been filed concerning real estate, involving either the title to the property or a claimed ownership interest in it. **Challenges ownership of property**

2. **Notice to Perform**- a notice to perform is a document that sets up contractual expectations for either the buyer or the seller. If the expectations are not met, then the deal can be canceled. The notice to perform gives one party a chance to remedy the situation before the deal can be canceled by the other party.

3. **Specific Performance** – specific Performance asks the court to force the opposing party into a contract that binds them to actually perform the contract at issue, rather than award damages for breach of contract. In real estate litigation, a buyer can force a reluctant seller to live up to the purchase and sale agreement.

B. Arbitration

ARBITRATION- *a form of alternative dispute resolution (ADR), is a legal technique for the resolution of disputes outside the courts. The parties to a dispute refer it to one or more persons (the "arbitrators", "arbiters," or "arbitral tribunal"), whose decision (the "award") they agree to be bound. It is a settlement technique in which a third party reviews the case and imposes a decision that is legally binding for both sides.*

1. Terms for Arbitration are listed on most Contracts

2. Make Request to solve issue with other side

3. Confirm receipt from opposing side

4. If terms can't be reached independently you will have to hire independent arbitration company, you can google companies and reviews

5. If an agreement cannot be reached through arbitration or if one party doesn't respond the plaintiff can proceed to court filings

ABBREVIATIONS AND ACRONYMS:

ARV: After repair value

CAP: Capitalization

CMA: Comparative Market Analysis

COCR/CCR/CoC: Cash on return

COF: Cost of funds

CRE: Commercial Real Estate

DSCR/DCR/DSR: Debt Service Coverage Ratio

FMR: Fair market rent

FMV: Fair market value

FSBO: For sale by owner

GRM: gross rent multiplier

HML: hard money lender

HOA: homeowners association

HUD: Federal Department of Housing and Urban Development

IRR: internal rate of return

JV: joint venture

L/O: lease option

LLC: limited liability company

LLP: limited liability partnership

MDU: multiple-dwelling unit

MFH: multi family home

MLS: Multiple Listing Service

NNN: triple-net lease

NOI: Net Operating Income

NOO: non-owner occupied

O/F: owner finance

OO: owner-occupied

P&S: purchase and sale

PCF: price-to-cash-flow ratio

POA: property owners association

REI: real estate investing

REIT: real estate investment trust

REO: real estate owned

ROI: return on investment

RTO: rent to own

SFH: single-family home

UW: Underwriter

ABOUT THE AUTHOR

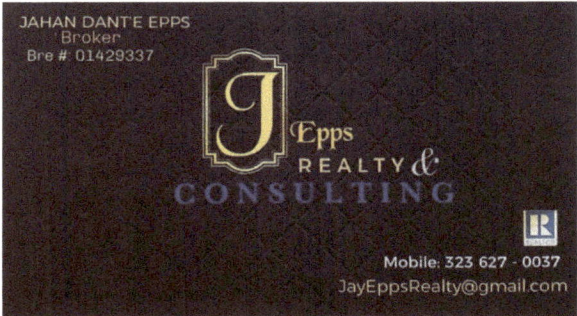

JAHAN DANTE EPPS
Broker
Bre # 01429337

J Epps
REALTY &
CONSULTING

Mobile: 323 627 - 0037
JayEppsRealty@gmail.com

www.ingramcontent.com/pod-product-compliance
Lightning Source LLC
Chambersburg PA
CBHW040931210326
41597CB00030B/5257